How to keep fit

by one who never is
as fit as he would like to be

By the same author

Flight narratives:
SOLO TO SYDNEY, 1930
ALONE OVER THE TASMAN SEA, 1933:
republished 1945 and 1966
RIDE ON THE WIND, 1937, republished 1967

Sailing narratives:
ALONE ACROSS THE ATLANTIC, 1961
GIPSY MOTH CIRCLES THE WORLD, 1967

Autobiography:
THE LONELY SEA AND THE SKY, 1964

Navigation:
ASTRO-NAVIGATION (four volumes), 1940–42
PINPOINT THE BOMBER (a game for teaching navigation), 1942
also a Planisphere, a Sun Compass and a Star Compass, 1942–44
THE POCKET MAP AND GUIDE OF LONDON

Anthology with Commentary:
ALONG THE CLIPPER WAY, 1966

How to keep fit

by one who never is as fit as he would like to be

Francis Chichester

b 1902.

HODDER AND STOUGHTON

First printed 1969
SBN 340 10955 6

Printed in Great Britain for Hodder and Stoughton Limited,
St. Paul's House, Warwick Lane, London, E.C.4, by
C. Tinling and Co. Limited, Liverpool, Prescot and London.

Contents

Acknowledgments

The exercise photographs were taken one afternoon in March 1968 on board the MV *Port Nelson* while on passage to New Zealand. The Nikonos camera which I used to take pictures (including the cover picture of this book) during my circumnavigation 1966–7 had broken down, but fortunately Eric Cockcroft, a fellow passenger, came to my rescue. He not only lent me his camera which would take my film and with which I photographed him doing the exercises, but he also took a set of me doing the exercises. These were only intended as guides for a professional photographing a gorgeous model doing the exercises later. However, the publishers wished to use the ones of the author, so here they are. I think Eric Cockcroft did a professional job anyway and I am most grateful to him.

This little book has been much harder to write than I had expected, and I thank John Anderson for giving me invaluable help in advising me what to leave out of my tale of woe covering the year of my life since I finished my circumnavigation; also Robin Denniston and Mark Hodder-Williams for checking both the exercises I recommend and my descriptions of them.

Lastly I thank my friends who checked my statements about the human body and health, especially Gordon and Barbara Latto, the two wise doctors and Anne Latto, of the Keep Fit Association.

Part I

I Introduction

This book chiefly describes a set of exercises which have been invaluable in keeping me fit or in helping me regain fitness after an accident or illness. I have written this description of my keep-fit regime in the hope that it will help others to improve their health and achievements.

I would like to be as fit as a tiger in the prime of life. I don't mean that I want to be able to carry a full-size bullock in my jaws without it touching the ground for four miles, but I would like to have a tiger's agility, endurance, speed, sight and hearing, and, perhaps I might add, its grace of movement. Alas, that species of animal, man, with all its brains, ingenuity and vaunted superiority over other animals, seldom succeeds in producing a member of the species as healthy as an average dog or cat. This is due to generations of unhealthy living, sitting still in tense concentration for hours at a time, stuffing ourselves with a lot of unsuitable food we don't really need, and enraging our livers with alcohol (as I enjoy doing, I must confess).

I have had many struggles to get fit again after accidents or illnesses, but at times in my life I have been wonderfully fit, bursting with vitality and pent-up desires for action. I owe a lot to exercises and other forms of physical training. I started doing exercises sixty years ago, and I have tried out many different systems of exercises and forms of training for sports, such as long distance running, boxing and Rugby football. At times I have lived a most active physical life. Besides playing a number of different games, ski-ing and skating, I have been a timber-mill worker, bushwhacker, fireman, gold-digger and coal-miner, and worked on a dairy farm, a sheep station and a cattle farm. Each of these sports and occupations is likely to use one set of muscles too much and leave the others neglected. I am now satisfied that my simple set of daily exercises provides one of the best ways of keeping fit in the difficult conditions of a crowded modern urban life. For years I used to swim every morning, winter and summer, or go for a run; often both. Either of these simple activities can have strange hazards; I can still see in my imagination that livid seventeen-foot octopus caught in the swimming bath at Wellington, New Zealand, just before I dived in; and I well remember one early morning in the war when, running across Hyde Park in the dark, I fell a purler into a bomb crater which had not been there the previous morning.

My regime chiefly consists of exercising for not more than half an hour every morning. It is not intended to build up muscle, speed or skilful movement. I think it can best be likened to the stretching, arching and yawning of a cat or dog on awakening. If we lived as natural a life as an animal, the same short stretching and arching as they do would keep us in the same comfortable state of well-being, fitness and agility. But we must make more effort than a cat to keep as fit. The primary objective of these exercises is the same as the cat-stretching

—to free every muscle and joint without strain and make the whole body supple.

People who know me or have read my accounts of flying and sailing adventures know that I have been ill several times and they may wonder why I write about fitness. I wondered if the title of this book should have been, "How to keep fit by one who never is", omitting "as fit as he would like to be". On considering my string of ailments, the most important thing I note is that up-to-date I have recovered each time. I believe that my regime of exercises, naturopathic treatment and diet have been powerful factors in my recovery and to-day I consider them the most potent factors I know. Also I have found, on examining the ailments, that they were all due to stress of one sort or another, or accidents or faulty diet. As I believe that most people nowadays have to undergo periods of illness due to stress, I have described briefly later in the book the events which caused the stresses leading to illness, and how I recovered each time. I only hope this may be of help to fellow-sufferers.

I must add, however, that I am no doctor and have no qualifications to prescribe for anyone else. I can only describe my own experiences and observations.

2 Ills, ailments and accidents

Unless one gets the plague, a pox or some other infectious disease, most illnesses, I believe, are caused by stress, chiefly emotional stress. The exceptions are the illnesses or damage due to accidents. For instance, it was an accident when an adder bit me and nearly finished me off at the age of eleven. Now I wonder if the poison from the adder or the antidote pumped into me to counteract it has been responsible for my violent allergy to aspirin since then, as when I was sent to the Marlborough College Hospital for mumps after being given an aspirin; and at other times I have become partially deaf, dumb and blind after being given one.

An accident can give a valuable lesson. When I was a boy I used to go off all day on my own, running through the woods of North Devon looking for birds' nests. The excitement lay in first finding a nest in an apparently inaccessible place and then reaching it. I was not particularly interested in getting an egg, except as a trophy. One day I fell about forty feet from the top of an oak tree which had no branches up the bottom half of the trunk. First I was hitting one branch after another, till I fell free. I crumpled up when I hit the ground and stayed there without making the slightest movement for what seemed a long time, while I wondered what damage was causing the pain. About ten minutes later I moved and was astonished to find that no bones were broken. I had lain there completely relaxed and since then, whenever I have had a bad fall, I have done the same thing—relaxed completely, and found that surprisingly often I have come out of it undamaged.

When I was seventeen I went to work on a farm in Leicestershire for five shillings a week. It seemed to me like a life of slavery, with only one half day's holiday in seven months, and long hours of work. Since I had to milk all those cows in the dark before the day's work, and again in the dark after the day's work, I have never been happy about drinking milk. While I was at this job I got bad rheumatism in my shoulders and when I woke each morning I would be unable to lift my arms above my shoulders. This may have been caused by the hard manual work, such as loading 200-lb. bags of wheat on to a dray by myself, but I do not think so; I think it was due to the stress of being unhappy. The only time I was happy during this period was after I had marvellous dreams at night, which I used to think about happily during the day.

For the next ten years I kept pretty fit, though mostly I ate quite the wrong food. Once, when I was left alone on the 2,000-acre sheep station which I and one other man looked after, I ate half a sheep in a week. Now that I prefer vegetarian food, I can at least claim that it is after thoroughly trying out both meat and vegetarian diets.

Between the ages of eighteen and twenty-eight it should not matter what rubbish one eats. A young person should have enough puppy fat and inborn healthiness to survive. During that time of my life I was, at first, leading an outdoor life: farming, saw-milling, coal-mining, bush-felling and gold-digging. Even after I became a businessman at the age of twenty-one I was out in the open a lot of the time, tramping over our properties, watching road-building and tree-planting and things of that sort. And when at twenty-seven I was half-owner of a small aviation company I still moved about a lot in the open air. But there was a good deal of nervous wear and tear due to our business, and it was building up.

When I was twenty-seven I had a busy year. After taking a steamer passage across the Pacific to America, I had demonstration flights in the best light planes available there. I was looking for the most reliable and, particularly, the most foolproof plane possible. By foolproof I meant easy to handle, responsive, and with no naughty tricks. My theory was that with such a plane one would be able to get out of difficulties and avoid accidents in emergencies which might well be fatal with a more tricky design. In England I finished learning to fly and went solo for the first time on the 13th August. On the 25th October I went for a trial flight round Europe by way of Yugoslavia, Rumania and Poland. On the 20th December I left Croydon for Sydney. At that time Hinkler was the only pilot to have flown this route solo. I would have liked to beat his time for the passage, but in the end I was glad enough to arrive intact. I was startled by the reception in Sydney, where ten aeroplanes escorted me in, and several thousand people waited for me on Mascot Airfield.

The fame I ran into hit me like a shock. A month after reaching New Zealand I was on the verge of a nervous breakdown. I do not believe it was due to the flying or to the string of adventures of the past year. Certainly a long solo flight was a tough project then. This may seem incredible now to people who are flown to Sydney in a few hours without effort, but in 1929 that route had only been taken solo once before: many landing grounds along it were tiny and some were dangerous; it was difficult to know in advance if their grass surfaces were usable, or a sea of mud which would tip the aeroplane on to its nose in monsoon weather; it was not easy to get information about the weather ahead; the dealings with airport, customs and other authorities, and with the suppliers of fuel, food and stores were long and tedious and I usually had to go through them twice a day, sometimes in different countries. In the open cockpit of the Gipsy Moth my head would be in the 90 m.p.h. slipstream for up to twelve hours a day. I certainly was fagged out when I reached Australia, but I am sure this was not the cause of my nervous exhaustion; it was due to the unexpected publicity bringing contact with thousands of new people. I shrank from such meetings.

When out walking, the personality of a stranger going in the opposite direction would strike me from some yards away and make a more or less painful impact according to its forcefulness. A doctor prescribed regular doses of Luminal for my nerves. I took refuge behind a black beard which seemed to hide and protect me, for I felt as if the nerves all over my body had been stripped of their covering tissue.

Recently I read a biography of Amy Johnson, who flew solo along the same route some months after me and who triggered off a global explosion of heroine-hysteria. Amy was afterwards told by her doctor that she was on the verge of insanity. I can well believe it.

As soon as I got back to New Zealand I wrote a book. I thought it would get the nightmares out of my system, but perhaps it would have been better to do nothing for a while. I walked only at night for exercise, and fetched drums of sea-water to bathe and soothe my nerves.

Looking back, with my present knowledge, I am sure I would have recovered much quicker had I run through my present keep-fit regime every day. It would have been invaluable during the actual flight; but at that time it would have seemed a ridiculous idea to do exercises during an incessant struggle against time. Now I believe it might easily have speeded up the flight by making me more efficient. 'If youth but knew, if age but could.'

However, my ambitions were needling me. Within six months, before my twenty-ninth birthday, I was hard at it preparing for a much more difficult flight. I wanted to complete a solo circumnavigation of the world and the first stage of this was to fly across the Tasman Sea from New Zealand to Australia. This flight, which to-day seems no more exciting than an airborne bus-ride, was to be the greatest adventure of my life because of the difficulty, the danger, the unknown hazards and the excitement. Briefly the difficulties were as follows: it was the first attempt to fly solo over the route and this introduced the unknown factors which always go with a first attempt at anything. The distance, two-thirds of the width of the Atlantic between Ireland and Newfoundland, was not great, but it was too much for the range of my Gipsy Moth. I had to make three hops of it, there being fortunately two islands in between. There was nowhere to land a plane on these islands and as no aeroplane had ever been seen there before, it was not safe to ask for a landing strip to be cleared, and I decided to turn the Gipsy Moth into a seaplane. This meant that I had to learn to fly a seaplane, which required a fresh technique with a lot of new problems. For example, it called for a lot of skilful seamanship; and there were the problems of alighting and taking off a seaplane weighing, with floats, only 1,100 lbs., from the open Pacific Ocean at Norfolk Island. As no-one had yet made a long distance flight alone in a seaplane, I had to foresee the likely problems such as anchoring or mooring, re-fuelling, servicing the engine while moored off, etc. There was a lot of sport and excitement in all this, but a lot of strain too. The biggest difficulty of all was to find these islands. There were no direction-finding radio facilities, so I set to work to devise a system of navigation for locating the islands by sextant observations of the sun. Such a thing had never been done before, even with a crew (and as far as I know has never been done since on solo flights—no doubt because radio and electronic aids have become available since then). My new system of navigation had to be accurate, because Lord Howe Island was only 3,500 acres, which subtended an angle of less than half a degree from my point of departure, and, as I could only carry nine hours' fuel for a flight, which, in the event, took seven hours forty minutes, there was no chance of returning or flying on elsewhere if I failed to find my target.

I had now been living to the full for two years, but in spite of the nervous exhaustion I had not had any organic illness. At one time towards the end of 1930, when I was beginning to feel desperate with so many obstacles to overcome, I took to a tent in the bush on our property and spent a fortnight felling trees in the scorching heat. I sweated away the poison of worry until I was bursting with vitality and felt that I could achieve anything; then returned to the fray. For a while it seemed as though the difficulties were insuperable. I felt I was being shot at with a double-barrelled shotgun; even if I could avoid the first barrel, loaded with all the difficulties and obstacles to my starting at all, I should then have to face the second barrel-full of the hazards and hardships of the actual flight. The strain was terrific. Early in 1931 I was suddenly attacked by severe illness. Excruciating pain was caused by the slightest movement of any joint or part of my body. I could leave my bed only by crawling on hands and knees. I was taken into Auckland General Hospital, where I was told that nothing could be found wrong to cause this illness; the doctors did not know what it was. I believe it was nature's way of making me rest; I had to, when I could not move. After a few days I simply recovered.

I escaped from the hospital and I did start the flight. My system of navigation worked, which was extremely lucky for me because Lord Howe Island was hidden in a rainstorm and I did not sight it until I was five miles from it. I do not wish for any series of adventures more exciting and thrilling than that flight across the Tasman Sea provided. It was deeply satisfying, not only because the navigation succeeded, but also because we rebuilt the seaplane more or less successfully when it was sunk to the bottom of the lagoon at Lord Howe Island by a gale during the night, while I was asleep ashore.

I had no more health troubles on account of this flight, though I was greatly inconvenienced by having the top of a finger torn off by the hook of a crane lifting the seaplane off the water in Australia. I left Sydney to continue my seaplane flight northwards in my attempt to complete the first solo flight round the world.

I had a most wonderful flight for 2,000 miles over the Great Barrier Reef along the coast of Australia and then over New Guinea to the Celebes, the Philippines, Formosa, China and Japan. I think I may well have experienced the best that flying could offer. I had all the interesting, exciting problems and adventures of taking a seaplane alone to many places where an aircraft had never even been seen at that time. Perhaps now I tend to recall only the delights and forget the pangs and difficulties.

My solo circumnavigation attempt, started in London in 1929, came to a grisly halt in a little out-of-the-way seaside harbour in Japan. The Japanese were ultra-sensitive about spies at that time and thought that I was one. They ordered me to alight in this tiny fishing harbour and nowhere else. There were a number of steel telephone lines stretched across the northern end of the harbour between two hilltops, and after I had taken off and was heading for Tokyo, I flew into these lines. Wires of a long span are invisible when one is flying fast, just as a roadside fence made of palings spaced apart will disappear from view when seen from a fast car. When the little Gipsy Moth seaplane flew into the wires, they took up the strain and catapulted it backwards. One or more of the wires cut through some of the struts holding the floats to the fuselage, hooked up behind the struts and catapulted the seaplane forwards again. As soon as the wires became taut, the seaplane was stopped, one float was torn off in the air and the seaplane was catapulted vertically downwards to hit the harbour wall. It must have been an extraordinary accident to watch; I am only sorry that I wasn't on the ground to watch it. When I became conscious, I thought I was dead and in heaven. I think this was chiefly because of the unearthly red twilight which was all I could see. The explanation was simple enough, I was looking through blood. Later I counted thirteen wounds or breaks. I was a physical and nervous wreck.

Although I was extremely tired by the time I had coaxed the seaplane up to Japan, I do claim that my complete nervous exhaustion was largely due to the strain caused by thousands of sympathetic Japanese filing past my hospital bed in the polite way for which Japan is famous. I got into a state where it was agony if the Japanese nurse (who, incidentally, was a police nurse) pulled out a single hair when dressing my wounds. I was somewhat consoled by an English-speaking visitor who told me how he had been reproached by a Japanese nurse for wincing while his wound was being sewn up. "A Japanese would never show that he was being hurt," she said. To which he replied, "Yes, and I expect a Hottentot would positively like it."

Six months later, when I was back in England, I still could not travel in a train unless I frequently looked out of the carriage window to make sure that there was no other train about to run into it from behind. Rushing into a tunnel was hell.

Luckily for me there had been a wonderfully skilful Japanese doctor in the next town, ten miles away, when I crashed and he had looked after me. But he could not understand English and I could not speak Japanese; perhaps this was why I did not realise at the time how badly damaged my spine was. For ten years it ached at times and because of it my personality was feeble. I often had a strong wish, which sometimes felt like a definite need, to stand on my head, something I had never learned to do. I suppressed this urge as a sign of incipient eccentricity. It was not until years later, when I began to run through a regime of exercises every morning, that I learned how to stand on my head. I am convinced that it was due to this and other exercises for stretching the spine that from then on I had no more spine trouble.

I believe that if only I had been doing my own set of exercises up to that crash, I could have recovered my shrivelled personality and started living fully again in a quarter of the time actually taken.

While I was recovering at Instow in North Devon, I wrote a book about my Tasman Sea adventure, and later while living by myself in a hut in the native forest at the top of our New Zealand property, I wrote another book, *Ride on the Wind*, about my flight from Sydney to Japan.

3 War

It was not until five years after my crash that I flew again, this time through twenty-two countries with a friend as passenger, from Sydney to London by way of Peking, Hanoi and Simla. Again I had exciting adventures; but this time I escaped health trouble, owing, I believe, to the flight attracting no publicity when we landed in England.

Soon after landing, I met Sheila and we got married. We went out to New

Zealand by steamer but could not settle there and came back to England, where for six months I searched fruitlessly for a job. Finally Arthur Hughes created a job for me as navigation specialist in his firm, Henry Hughes & Son, makers of navigation instruments for a hundred years.

I used to start work at five a.m. writing articles and books on navigation to increase my income enough to make ends meet—my pay of £8.13.0 per week did not cover the rent of our Chelsea flat. I found it a hard life working regular office hours and taking orders from several bosses, after having been in business on my own since I was twenty-one. I think it was due to unhappiness or emotional stress that I was laid low with gallstone trouble just before the 1939 war broke out. I have been told that passing such a stone can be one of the most painful things known to man. Fortunately one loses consciousness when pain reaches a certain level of intensity. My wife refused to let the surgeons cut me open and after a spell in hospital, followed by a strict diet etc., I recovered.

I tried three times to get into the Air Force but was always turned down because of my bad sight and age. I thought I was in the prime of life at thirty-eight and I had acute vision with the help of spectacles. For instance, one morning I had shot five running rabbits with a rifle and I reckoned that must be a useful skill for a fighter pilot. Also I had done a lot of tricky flying. The country was desperately in need of pilots at the beginning of the Hitler War and I felt fed up. Perhaps I was trying too hard.

However, some time after the War had started I was sent for and put into uniform, and I wrote about navigation instruction for the first half of the War. After a time I was forcing myself to write and think when I was longing to be in action. I began to have a pain which appeared to be dyspepsia. It increased and nagged at me until frequently it would grow too intense and I would have to stop work and lie down for a while. At the end of this chairborne period I had written six books, produced a planisphere, a simple star compass, a simple sun compass, a game for teaching dead-reckoning navigation and a star chart, besides writing, I reckoned, half a million words of navigation instruction for the Royal Air Force.

In the end I became so stale and stagnant that I was sent away from the Air Ministry. I was offered a posting to the Empire Central Flying School if I would drop in rank to Pilot Officer. After ten days there, the Commandant appointed me Chief Navigation Officer. This was a Wing Commander's post but I was not allowed to hold that rank because I was not officially allowed to fly at all, owing to my eyesight. Fortunately the Commandant believed in getting on with the war at all costs and said I could fly solo or as crew as much as I wished, in order to do my job efficiently. So, for the second half of the war, I had an intensely interesting job devising new methods of navigation training, with plenty of flying and navigation. In addition I had a daily run on waking and plenty of sport thrown in, so that I became fully relaxed, happy and fit. This was the first time since I was eighteen that I had had no responsibility except to do my job to the best of my ability, with no worry about having to make money or fulfil ambitions. I was certainly as full of vitality as I had ever been. Was this due to my living the life which best suited me or for which I had an instinct?

After the War I started my map-publishing business from scratch. I had to learn and earn as I went along. At first I was the only person in the firm; I not only designed, produced and sold the maps, parcelled them up and delivered them, but also kept the books, invoiced the goods and typed the letters. I was full of optimism and intended to divide my time between my map business in England and my land-plantation business in New Zealand, flying myself out to New Zealand and back once a year in a light plane. I soon found that starting the business was a slow struggle for financial survival. Often I thought with despair that I would never succeed and would be stuck for ever in an office chair. At times I was desperate with money worries. I lost my health and the gallstone trouble returned. A doctor, urgently summoned, wanted to operate immediately, but once again my wife was convinced that this would be the wrong thing to do. It was then that I met Dr. Gordon Latto, who had become so impressed by the efficacy of nature-cure methods that he had switched over almost completely from his orthodox practice to natural healing. He said that he could stop the gallstones from forming, but that I must go on a strict vegetarian diet for a year, besides knocking off drink and smoking (which he said was worse than drink). This was a tough regime; the gallstones could not survive it. I did, however, and at the end of the period I found that I was cured of smoking, and that the vegetarian diet suited me so well that I have preferred it ever since.

Soon I was really fit again. This may have been helped by an improvement in my business and the consequent easing of worry. I had gradually been making bigger and better maps during the struggle for financial survival. Slowly the business had grown and had begun to take an original form. My New Zealand partner, Geoffrey Goodwin, on a visit to England, made a valuable suggestion that I should produce my picture map of London in the form of a small pocket map. For two years this looked like being a flop, and I nearly dropped it, but in the end it succeeded.

By 1951 I was again fit and tingling with vitality. The only physical defect that I had was bad eyesight and, puffed up with optimistic cockiness, I decided that I must cure it.

I have pretty severe myopia and astigmatism. People with normal sight may wonder what it is like to have bad sight. My own short sight is like looking through a powerful magnifying glass held close to a normal eye and the effect of the astigmatism is to see several overlapping images of a crescent moon instead of one. On several occasions my dearest ambition at the time had been dashed to the ground by bad sight. It had prevented me as a boy from entering the Navy and at Marlborough College, when I was crazy about rugby, it had seriously handicapped me. I remember once losing sight of a ball punted high up in the air, and running hard in the wrong direction for it. After that I was crazy about boxing and at nineteen wanted to turn professional; but a boxer who could not see the whites of his opponent's eyes could never be in the champion class. Later, bad sight menaced my flying ambitions. At the start I was not allowed the elementary amateur pilot's 'A' Licence unless I wore special goggles prescribed by the Air Ministry. (I never did wear these because I could not see well through them and they would have been dangerous.) Later I coveted the commercial pilot's 'B' Licence to enable me to carry paying passengers; but a 'B' Licence was quite impossible without perfect sight. In the end I was granted one, but it was only as a special privilege after I had flown alone from England to Australia. I have already described how I was turned down as a fighter pilot in the War and was not allowed to fly officially at all because of my bad sight.

By 1951, when I determined to try and cure my bad sight, I had read several books advocating different methods of eye treatment. The problem was to change the diameter of my eyeballs to cure the short sight and to alter the shape of them to cure the astigmatism. For fifteen months I gave my eyes the full treatment, morning, day and evening. This consisted chiefly of focusing and neck exercises with a lot of blinking, splashing the eyeballs with cold water, straining to see through the blur of short sight and resting the eyes frequently in the palms of my hands. One book considered that a vegetarian diet was an important factor.

I want to stress how fit I was at this time. As soon as I got up I used to run three miles across the parks and swim in the Serpentine, winter or summer. Several times a week I went to the skating rink for ice dancing. Sometimes I shadow-boxed and once a year I had a ski-ing holiday. At weekends I went shooting or fishing or bicycling. It was wonderful to feel so fit.

Now the sad sequel; my health began to fail. I had catarrh and for month after month could not get rid of it. I slipped a disc while shadow-boxing. I began to have nasty pains which I feared were due to some dreadful disease but which were eventually diagnosed as internal cramps due to nervous exhaustion. I carried on regardless but one morning, on returning from my run to the Serpentine, my lungs seized up. I could not breathe. It never occurred to me that this was simply a bad attack of asthma. I realised that I was getting weaker but kept on with the eye drill. What I did not realise was that my ailments were due to nervous exhaustion caused by the sight experiment. The incessant effort of trying to force the eyeballs into a different shape was too great a strain. Occasionally I had been able to see well for a fraction of a second, which had filled me with hope.

The following winter I went on my ski-ing holiday at St. Anton without spectacles. I have done lots of stupid things in my life but I think this takes the cake. I fell badly and broke my ankle. Suddenly, after fifteen months of it, I realised that my sight-cure experiment was futile and that my ailments were all due to it. I had my sight measured by an optician and the astigmatism was unchanged; the short sight had only improved a fraction from four to three and a quarter diopters. What a failure! Next day I started wearing spectacles again, and three months later my sight was the same as it had been before, but I was fit, strong and happy. I, a member of that much-vaunted animal species, homo sapiens, would have to put up with the ridiculous disability of balancing a pair of spectacles on my human nose before I could see as well as a cat.

4 I take up sailing

By 1953 I had become desperate to navigate again. I decided to go in for sailing and took up ocean racing as the best means of learning quickly. I still had financial worries and fits of despair during frequent bad business spells. To this strain I now added the effort of learning to sail and ocean-race from scratch. On looking back I am astonished how ignorant I was when I started ocean-racing; my only experience of the seamanship and navigation required was what I had gained in seaplane handling and air navigation. I learnt quickly because there is nothing like an emergency or a tricky situation for teaching fast and driving the lesson home; and I had my full share of emergencies. To increase the tension I picked for crew men who knew as little or even less than I did.

The time came when *Gipsy Moth II* was racing across the North Sea and one of the crew who claimed to have sailed a lot had been exasperating the rest of us throughout the race. Finally he did something which I thought was particularly stupid and which infuriated me. I felt something like a hot splash spreading in my belly under my ribs, as if something had burst inside me. A few days later, sailing back to England, I began to feel ill and was soon in agony. I was glad on this occasion to have a crew so that I could crawl into my bunk, though I believe that I would have escaped the whole trouble if I had been sailing single-handed.

Later in the season I was becoming a sick man, but I was determined, if I possibly could, to race *Gipsy Moth II* in my first Fastnet Race, whatever the cost. The race took six days, and before it ended I had to be helped out of my bunk to the cockpit, and had difficulty in holding on to the chart while navigating. I went to a big London hospital where a specialist, after examining the X-ray pictures, said that I was a typical case of chronic arthritis. I certainly was in a bad way; I could not open a door without great difficulty, even using two hands, and once I dropped a full plate of soup over myself because I was unable to hold it. After some weeks of treatment at the hospital, Dr. Latto said to me, "Ask your fellow patients how long they have been receiving this treatment, and then decide for yourself whether it seems likely to cure you." This made me think hard, and as a result I asked him to prescribe nature-cure treatment for me. I took a severe course and then went to Edstone, a nature-cure place. I was in such a state that after I had sat down on the ground on a fine autumn day, I was unable to get to my feet again. I had to wait until someone happened along to pull me up. Fortunately, the treatment succeeded; it appeared to take a long time, but to me it seemed miraculous that by the following spring I was cured and once again racing hard in *Gipsy Moth II.*

By the end of 1957, my fourth season's ocean-racing, I was again in serious trouble with my health. Dr. Arthur Guirdham, in his book, *Cosmic Factors in Disease,* maintains that most illness is due to strain or stress, usually caused by living at the direction of the intellect instead of the instinct. Also by trying too hard and planning to fulfil ambitions instead of living in the present and, if I understand the book aright, doing what comes naturally.

I had had a tough year in the office and a lot of worry, besides a hard season's sailing. I raced my own *Gipsy Moth II* in three RORC events, and at the end of the English Channel Race in my own yacht I jumped aboard *Figaro,* a crack American yacht, to navigate it for the owner, Bill Snaith, in a series of races for the Admiral's Cup. There were four races for this Cup, including the Fastnet Race. Then, after that, Bill asked me to navigate his *Figaro* from Plymouth to London Docks for shipping to America, and that was a very exciting ride. We averaged 5½ knots all night, running dead up-Channel under bare poles; I wouldn't have missed it for anything.

All that year I had had tremendous worry and work in connection with the business. On top of that, at the start of the year my wife had persuaded me to put in hand a new yacht, *Gipsy Moth III.* Besides the designing and building of the boat, there was the financing to worry about. I had not got the money to pay for it, but my wife said, "Have faith and go ahead." Throughout the year I was worrying about my business, and alternated between bouts of despair at the liability of the new yacht and waves of enthusiasm for it. Lastly, I had the worry of trying to sell *Gipsy Moth II.* Every weekend I went down to work on her, tidying up the mess left after the season's racing. I worked feverishly. One of my jobs was to remove some old paint on the floor of the forecastle. I was using a strong chemical paint remover, working on my knees and doubled up over the stuff on the floor. The forehatch was closed above my head because of the cold. For a long time after this I believed that the fumes burnt my lungs, and that my lung trouble started then. Now, I think there may have been another cause: that I was in bad condition, run down, and flooding my body with poisons distilled from negative feelings—despair, resentment, bitterness, fear, worry and exhaustion. These are the causes of most functional illnesses. I began to cough. I retired to my little room at the top of our house. Then followed pleurisy, an abscess in my lung, and pneumonia, one after the other. It wasn't long before I was told to enter a big hospital for my lung to be removed because of cancer. The surgeon told me that he thought it was already too late to operate. It was my only possible hope, he said. I think I must repeat what I wrote* after hearing what seemed to be a death sentence:

"Half a year had passed since I was first ill, and when I emerged from the hospital" (after hearing the above verdict) "it was a fine spring morning in April. As I walked along, the sun shone in my face. I heard the gay spring song of birds. Young pale green leaves were beginning to tint the trees. Life had never seemed more wonderful—a priceless, desirable thing to lose. My body seemed empty, my bones full of water. It was like a nightmare where I was in a bottomless space of loneliness. I had read about this sort of thing happening to other people; somehow I had never imagined that it would happen to me. I walked along slowly, wondering how long I had got before I was snuffed out from this lovely fresh spring life."

My wife took what seemed to me the incredibly courageous course of refusing to allow my lung to be removed. The chief surgeon said that she was wasting valuable time, destroying my only chance of living. But she stuck to her opinion that my lungs were in such a septic state that I was bound to die if they were cut into.

The thing in my lung did not grow. I believe that a strange factor in my keeping alive was the look in my friends' eyes when they came to visit me; they obviously thought they were seeing me for the last time. This spurred me on to make another effort.

"I wanted only to lie still in peace and to defer the horrid moment when I would start coughing, and pass through the experience of feeling suffocated. There came a time when I said that suffocation had caused me to die a thousand deaths, but this was an exaggeration; perhaps it was a hundred, or even less. But it is what *seems* that counts, not what is. I had always heard that drowning was a pleasant death. I cannot understand this. Perhaps it is different to be choked by water from outside. I developed a terrified dread of that slow choking from within. I despised myself as I became an abject coward about dying that way. As each fresh crisis built up, I wanted to cry as if surrendering to that weakness would give me respite."

A month later my wife took me by car to Enton Hall, another nature-cure place. After the standard hospital diet, I was grateful for vegetarian food, with fresh fruit, and raw grated vegetables. I found that when it became difficult to breathe, a complete fast for two or three days made breathing a little easier. As soon as I discovered this, I repeated it whenever breathing became unbearably difficult. A strange situation now arose, for instead of being encouraged to fast, as is usual in a nature-cure hydro, I was being advised either not to do it or to cut it short because I had not the strength to stand it. There came a night when everyone gave up hope for me. My own doctor had driven down from London.

* *The Lonely Sea and the Sky.*

He told my wife that my heart was giving out under the strain. I knew that they had given me up that night and somehow it did me good. It enthused in me will to live. I think it was a crisis.

After surviving that night, I got a little better and was able to shuffle into the grounds. It was a gorgeous summer. I loved the warm touch of the sun on my skin, the rising scent of the pine needles, the soothing green of juicy, young, curled-up bracken fronds. I liked to watch a big ant-heap of large, fierce black-red ants at work.

I was able to go home, to the only place where I wanted to be, my room at the very top of the house, my cave, my kennel, where I could wrap a blanket round the remains of my shattered personality, and turn my face to the window.

I was cleared of cancer by now but my lungs were in a frightful state. They were nearly full of liquid at times with severe bronchitis and asthma. Perhaps I suffered most at this period, because I feared and dreaded the suffocation attacks and my personality had shrunk to almost nothing. This upsets people; they are used to someone having a certain personality, and if that alters, they feel he is a different person and they have to suppress a contempt for his changed state and weakness. My weight had dropped forty pounds and my skin hung in folds and was sometimes pinched against the bath by my bones.

About eighteen months after I was first taken ill, I had an almost irresistible urge to go to the south of France. I want to make it clear that by this time I had been passed as free of cancer by several doctors. However, in Vence I had a bad attack of bronchitis and asthma. I fell into the hands of Dr. Jean Mattei, a remarkable man, who treated me with some drugs which cleared up my condition in a few days' time. I think that this whole lung trouble was a stress effect brought on by my condition in 1957. It was something that came at me in waves, each wave building up to a crest and subsiding. By the time I reached France I was nearly at the end of it but there were still small waves of illness battering at my water-logged lung. After Jean's elixirs, I got better rapidly. Incidentally, my wife still asserts that it was not the drugs but the confidence and positive healing manner of the good doctor which were responsible for my amazing recovery from that particular wave of illness. I think it was the drugs.

Since this illness I have often been told by doctors and other people concerned with illness that I could not have had cancer, or that I could not have recovered if I had had it. I am no expert in this matter, but I can hardly believe that nine top lung surgeons, physicians, radiologists and a laboratory physicist could all have been wrong when they diagnosed lung cancer. I have seen a written report and listened to spoken reports of this diagnosis. It seems to me unfair for anyone who had not examined me at the time to criticise the opinions of men who had. The doctors were doing their best for me, for which I am most grateful.

Three months after visiting France I had recovered sufficiently to go as navigator in an off-shore race in the English Channel. Afterwards the owner of the yacht told me that he had been frightened by my condition; and I had to call in another French doctor when we reached St. Malo, but by then I had managed to navigate to the end of the race.

My health continued to improve slowly but steadily and in 1960, fifteen months after I had appealed to Dr. Mattei for oxygen in Vence, I was able to cross the starting line for the toughest yacht race that had yet taken place, the first Singlehanded Trans-Atlantic Race. This was not only the first time that the Atlantic had been raced across from east to west by small yachts, but also the first ocean singlehanded race anywhere in the world. I thoroughly enjoyed it. No doubt my enjoyment was heightened by *Gipsy Moth* being the winner, but it was the sort of adventure I loved. My health improved. Two years later I raced across the Atlantic alone again, this time on a record-breaking passage. And two years after that, in 1964, I took part in the second Singlehanded Trans-Atlantic Race, this time finishing second to the French lieutenant, Eric Tabarly. There was not the same magic in the second race as in the first. Without doubt there is a tremendous added thrill in doing anything for the first time. In 1960, that first race across the Atlantic had seemed hazardous and arduous—"three thousand miles, plugging into the prevailing westerlies, probably strong, bucking the Gulf Stream current, crossing the Grand Banks off Newfoundland, which are not only one of the densest foggy areas of the world but also stuffed with fishing trawlers and icebergs."* But, after a passage has proved possible, or a hitherto impossible flight has been achieved, these things lose some of their first spicy, adventurous tang. Now singlehanded races are springing up all round the world, and the North Atlantic seems to have shrunk.

5 The three-Cape circumnavigation

In 1966 a great new venture turned up. I was going to attempt a fast voyage round the world, along the old Clipper Way, round the three great Capes, Good Hope, Leeuwin and the Horn. This was the route which the gold clippers of the 1850s, and afterwards the wool and grain clippers, followed on their voyage out from England to Australia and then onwards round the world back to England. I wanted to make a fast passage, rivalling the average speed of the famous square-rigged clippers, but singlehanded in a 38-foot water-line, 10-ton boat compared with a 30-man crew in a 1,000-ton boat of 100-foot water-line. I was convinced —and I still am—that this old sailing route along the Clipper Way was the greatest challenge for a small boat and its crew that the world can provide (barring stunt voyages).

My objective was to equal the average time of the fastest clippers to Australia, which I set at one hundred days out, and one hundred and ten days home, and to complete the voyage round the world with only one stop. To achieve this speed, I planned non-stop passages out and back, the first of 14,100 miles and the second of 15,500 miles.

I suppose I could claim to have achieved the one hundred days out, because I was off Melbourne ninety-nine days out from Plymouth, and so could have made the passage to Melbourne in one hundred days; but I had set my heart on Sydney as my port of call. This cost me another eight days of slow, tough sailing without a self-steering gear to help me. The self-steering had broken in half 2,850 miles from Sydney. It might well have taken me even longer, which is indicated by the fact that the great *Cutty Sark*'s fastest passage to Sydney was ten days longer than her fastest passage to Melbourne.

The homeward passage took me one hundred and nineteen days. The yacht was knocked down in the Tasman Sea which cost me an extra week, and the departure from Sydney instead of Melbourne cost me several more days.**

* *The Lonely Sea and the Sky.*

** The clippers took longer on the homeward passage, but, to avoid long explanation, I said I was going to try for a one-hundred-day homeward passage.

I have been ill off and on throughout the year since I ended this voyage. In this keep-fit book I must offer an explanation; perhaps if I set out the facts, the cause will become clear.

By the spring of 1966 I had been training for months to get into peak condition for the voyage, and I was 'in the pink'.

I thought I could achieve my aim with careful planning and a boat specially designed for the task. I had been preparing for the voyage for three years and everything looked simple and easy; but, from the moment that the new boat, *Gipsy Moth IV*, was launched, things began to go wrong and worry started to build up. The yacht was so tender that in only a fresh breeze she would heel over and lie practically on her beam ends with masts horizontal. She had to be hauled ashore for more than a ton of lead to be added to the ballast keel. Even after that she was still so tender that I dreaded the thought of what would happen to her in the big, rough seas and strong winds of the Southern Ocean. My son, Giles, put the matter clearly when he said one needed a ladder to cross from one side of the deck to the other. However, I was committed to the venture and had to go on with it. One day when I was out alone on trials, I slipped on the wet glass of a skylight in the middle of the deck. My feet shot from under me and, owing to the heel of the boat, I came down crash on my thigh. Four days later, the pain began and I found my foot half paralysed. This partial paralysis, or if that is not the right word, complete loss of feeling and power of movement, attacked one part of my foot at a time. The small toes might be out of action, or at another time the big toe, or the outside of the foot, and so on. Like a fool I did not go to my doctor; the truth was I was frightened he would try to stop my voyage. I worked hard with exercises, trying to get back the movement in my foot and leg. It was a bad handicap, not so much because I had lost all balancing control in that leg, for I knew that I could get along on the boat without it, using my hands, and by pressing some part of my body against the mast or a shroud to keep balanced; but because I could not walk or do my daily exercises which are essential to keep me fit. Without my exercises and walking I soon get depressed and out of condition. Indeed, it was to be fifteen months before I could begin to walk enough to provide me with any real exercise.

Then Sheila had an accident. The doctor said her health was in such a serious state that she must go to bed straight away for three weeks' complete rest. I was deeply worried about her; she had been working too hard for months, not only on my venture, but also helping to run our map publishing business.

Then my fourth worry turned up; I had to find £12,000 towards the cost of the boat, in addition to the large sum which my cousin had so generously put up already. So all through the summer, when I had looked forward to spending time in sailing trials in all conditions of weather and sea, I was involved in difficult business dealings.

As a result of all this I started the voyage much less fit and prepared than I had hoped to be. No doubt this was a factor in my arriving exhausted in Sydney, but there were others: I had reckoned to do a lot of cooking on the passage, for which I had several vegetarian cookery books on board. This plan went adrift. *Gipsy Moth IV* was tough to handle and it took far more hard effort to keep her racing than I had allowed for. If I had been cruising I would have had plenty of spare energy, but as it was I was too tired to cook elaborate dishes. It even required an effort of will to bake periodically the wholemeal bread which was so important. I had relied on the cooking for protein and had not a sufficient supply of tinned fish, etc. to make good the deficiency. Then, all my eggs had gone bad earlier on the passage. Also, I had been taking a glucose preparation to provide me with a burst of energy for an emergency job such as handling a sail in the middle of the night when hit by a squall. The stuff achieved its object but seemed to kill my appetite, and I ate far less than I should have done of the available food left to me. As a result, I think I was half starved of protein. Then, at the end of the passage, I had a tough seven days' grind up the east coast of New South Wales against wind and a strong south-going current, without my self-steering gear to help me. On top of that I had been short of sleep for several nights owing to the closeness of the coast, having to tack to and fro across the shipping lane all night, plugging into a head wind. Lastly, it was not restful being escorted into Sydney by a fleet of craft of all sorts on the final day of the passage. I am not surprised that I was exhausted and looked like Methuselah trying to balance himself on his two legs as I stumbled ashore at the Sydney jetty.

At the end of the voyage, however, when I sailed into Plymouth Sound, I felt hardy, fit and healthy. For more than a month during a superb sail up through the North Atlantic, I had not only had no asthma, which had bedevilled me ever since my lung trouble in 1958, but I had even forgotten about it. My lame leg still gave me trouble, because I could not balance on it, and my elbow was painful with bursitis and two tiny chips off the bone; but these things were merely accidental. I certainly was tired when I landed, but that was nothing unusual—any crew of a small yacht is usually tired after an off-shore race of only 250 miles.

Stress and strain may have built up in me during the voyage without my knowing it. Dr. Guirdham states that "Many airmen or members of submarine crews live through their arduous experiences without showing nervous symptoms, only to break down when afforded rest." But I think that my health failed for quite another reason, the same one that had brought me to the edge of a nervous breakdown in 1930 after my solo flight to Australia.

6 And afterwards

As I write this, it is a year since I finished my voyage round the world. My health-story in that year, I think, illustrates very clearly the points I have tried to make in this book: that ill-health derives mainly from stress, strain and conditions of the mind, that good health can be achieved by the relief of stress.

When I sailed into Plymouth at the end of my voyage I had been alone for 119 days, close on four months. After such a period of solitude the impact of just one person is terrific. When I saw the slopes of the Sound black with people—the Lord Mayor of Plymouth estimated the number at about one quarter of a million— I felt a wave of alarm and depression: I thought, "My God, I have ruined my life with this voyage."

I had a tremendous and overpowering welcome, but immediately I landed I was involved in business worries. A week after landing in Plymouth I went on board *Gipsy Moth IV*, lying at her old mooring off Mashford's yard at Cremyll, and as I stepped into the cabin I suddenly felt dizzy. My sight shimmered and wavered like hot air over rock on a scorching summer day. I lay resting all afternoon, but I still felt something was wrong that evening, when we went off to dine with the Commander-in-Chief, Admiral Sir Fitzroy Talbot. Soon after I started to eat I knew that I was going to faint, and I asked my hostess if I might withdraw without disturbing the party. I lay down on top of a bed, and presently had a horrible, nightmarish feeling of the world shaking away beneath me and projecting me into infinite space, a frightening and lonely feeling. I wondered if I was dying, and, if so, why this should be. When I recovered consciousness I was lying on the floor, with people moving about in the twilight.

It turned out that I had a duodenal ulcer, and I ended up in the Royal Naval Hospital at Plymouth, where, first of all, three-quarters of a gallon of new blood was poured into my veins. The medical pundits said it was a good thing this had not happened while I was alone on the ocean. *I felt convinced that it would not have happened if I had stayed at sea.*

Why did I get this ulcer? Adelle Davis, in her book, *Let's Get Well,* reports Dr. Hans Selye as saying, "Ulcers have developed overnight in soldiers awaiting battle, or even in students apprehensive about exams." I think that my ulcer was due, firstly, to the strain of meeting so many people, and trying to understand all their feelings and viewpoints after four months of solitude, and secondly (perhaps chiefly) to the stress of business concerned with the yacht, and a renewal of all the financial worry I had before I set off on the voyage.

I spent four happy weeks in the Royal Naval Hospital after the initial anxiety had passed, and was fit enough to go straight from hospital on board *Gipsy Moth IV,* to sail to the Royal Naval College at Greenwich, where a tremendous honour awaited me—to be dubbed Knight by the Queen, using Sir Francis Drake's own sword. I must confess I was in a funk. The only way to avoid being paralysed and tongue-tied through nervous self-consciousness was to try to stop feeling altogether: if I once let my feelings loose, I should be paralysed by stage-fright. I tried to split my personality: I ordered the No. 1 me to be brave and act the part, while the No. 2 me remained the master, hovering and watching that the slave did his best. However, the Queen seemed to be relaxed and enjoying herself, and she was certainly very gracious to me; she even told me to wave to the people cheering.

Then there was a wonderful motorcade procession with the Lord Mayor of London through the City streets, for another huge reception, this time at the Mansion House. This was another tremendous honour; it was also a tremendous strain. From then on I had business to attend to, I had to get on with writing my book*, and it was a struggle not to be engulfed in a social maelstrom. My whole nature, which gets its satisfaction from things like solitary adventure, was tortured by intense social activity among strangers. Hundreds of invitations came to me, and if I did not accept—as often I could not accept—I dreaded appearing ungrateful or, perhaps, causing offence.

Soon after I tried to get down to work, I began to feel ill. Asthma started up again, followed by bronchitis. I began running a temperature. Soon I was spending more time in bed than out of it. There were some functions that I felt I *must* attend if I possibly could: I should have been ashamed if I had pulled out. For example, when I landed in Plymouth I had accepted an invitation to speak at a Boxing Dinner of the International Sporting Club, but had to pull out at short notice owing to my ulcer. This must have caused the Club trouble, and I

* *Gipsy Moth Circles the World* (Hodder & Stoughton). A print of 100,000 bound copies appeared on October 10, 1967, and the book was published in five languages before the end of the year.

hated the thought of causing still more trouble by cancelling again. I had an extra urge to go because when I was young I had such a craze for boxing. So I crawled out of bed for that function, and returned after it with a higher temperature. The same sort of thing happened several times. Again and again I tackled something because I felt I ought to do so, while my inner self was resenting it; I hardly recovered from being flattened out by one event before the next one made me ill again.

It seemed impossible in England to get the rest I had been warned I must have, so my wife and I went to Switzerland, where I hoped that a hideaway and scrambling among the mountains would put me right. But we ran into Press interviews and functions all along the route. My lungs grew worse. I got no joy from the lovely mountains. I longed to climb to the summit so that I could see all around, but I could not walk fifty metres at a time without a rest, gasping for breath, trying to extract more oxygen from the air, because my lungs were water-logged, or clogged up, except for a small part at the top.

After a miserable flight back to London, trying not to look ill, I was glad to kennel up again in my room at home. Here, with some drastic fasting and a strict nature-cure regime, I recovered slowly, and cut down the asthma and bronchitis until presently I felt fit again. I tackled business, but, unhappily, I had no reserve of nervous energy. As soon as I went off to another function or affair I was at once in trouble, and the dreary routine had to be endured again.

I decided that my only hope was a slow passage to New Zealand in a cargo ship, and in mid-January 1968 Sheila and I left Tilbury in the *Port Nelson.* I plugged away at my keep-fit exercises, and paced up and down the deck for several miles a day*, slowly recovering the balance and full use of my damaged leg. Between Panama and Samoa a small swimming pool was rigged on deck, and it was heaven to splash about in this two or three times a day. The balm of this sea-water swimming, which must surely be one of the finest cures for nervous exhaustion, combined with plenty of walking and exercises, began to make me fit and able to enjoy life again. Another month of this wonderful healing routine in the balmy tropics would have set me up completely. Alas, when we reached Samoa the swimming pool had to be dismantled because some of the cargo was stowed in the hold beside it. And the publicity pressure was turned on again. We had taken care not to tell anyone when or where we were going, but at every port the ship called at, Curaçao, Panama, Samoa, Suva, Larantoeka, it was the same routine, and meeting many strangers began to undo my recovery.

As soon as we steamed through the welcoming fleet of yachts at New Plymouth, New Zealand, and saw the crowds on the wharf, I realised that the idea of the voyage to New Zealand had been rather crazy. I had business to do connected with my old plantations in New Zealand, and this did not make things any easier. Once again my lungs got worse, and each day my activity was reduced until I was back to the old predicament of not being able to move more than a few yards at a time. I could not relax and recover living at a hotel.

So we flew to Australia, to spend our first week in Sydney at Admiralty House, the Governor-General's Sydney residence. Here we were in a sanctuary, in an old mansion on a lovely site, sloping down to the water's edge. I do not think there could be a more thoughtful, kindly hostess than Lady Casey. But after that first week of peace I was committed to a heavy list of activities, and I

* This was when the photographs were taken which illustrate the exercises in part II of this book.

knew that I was going to be too ill to move. In despair, I asked for help from a top asthma specialist. He top-dressed my lungs, pumped drug into my veins, and gave me another drug to swallow. Within a few hours I felt normal.

I was grateful for being enabled to get through my work, but I was not happy, because I was sure that suppression of symptoms in this way could result only in a reaction worse than the original illness, unless the respite could be used for rest and recuperative treatment— and this was impossible for me. The effect of the drugs wore off during the flight home, and by Singapore I was in serious trouble again. When, after another day's flight, we landed in Teheran at two a.m. I was in poor condition, could walk only with difficulty, and wondered if I would survive to reach home. Although it was the middle of the night, photographers and reporters were waiting. If you sail round the world alone you are expected to be as tough as an old boot, and people just seem unable to understand if you try to explain that at the moment you feel half-dead. I kennelled up at the hotel, eating nothing until we left two mornings later. I think the dry air at 4,500 feet helped, and I was better when we left. Our house in London, when we reached it, was like heaven—I imagine that a bird nesting in a tall tree must feel the same. I don't enjoy fasting, but I was grateful for the amazing good that a fast did me, and a week later I repeated the treatment. As soon as Dr. Gordon Latto thought me fit enough, he sent me off to hospital for a complete overhaul. This was the sort of jaunt I had dreaded since my cancer drama; something must be suspected. Fortunately, nothing new was discovered—except that I had lost a kidney. I was taken aback; I felt as if I had suddenly lost an old friend. This was nonsense, because it must have disappeared long ago. When and how? I wondered. Was it due to my fall from an upstairs window when I was a child, or, perhaps, to that forty-foot fall from a tree when birds'-nesting as a boy? Or maybe a kidney punch in one of my boxing fights had damaged it, or the air-crash in Japan. The doctors were more cheerful about my missing kidney than I was, and said it didn't matter (as long as no one cut out the remaining one, thinking that I had a spare!).

Gordon Latto declared that the time had come to get me completely well. I could not go on having one relapse after another, for I might end up with chronic bronchial asthma. He put me on a stiff nature-cure regime, which, with my run-through of exercises, took about three hours every day. I was to cancel all engagements, functions and business for three months. Already, after one month of this treatment, I look so well that it is difficult to convince my friends that I cannot join in parties, functions or business conferences. How difficult it is to be grateful for feeling fit after a bout of illness! All one's misery is forgotten as soon as it ends. What I take as a sure sign of having passed a health crisis is that I have started thinking out how *Gipsy Moth V* should be designed.

Part II

Keep-fit exercises

Although I am convinced that almost everyone will benefit from doing these exercises, I am not a doctor and have no qualifications to advise on health matters. What follows is the regime of exercises which, after sixty years' experience and trying out of many different systems, I have found most effective in keeping me fit.

The overall time for the exercises should not exceed thirty minutes. I do not like doing exercises and I cannot believe that anyone else does. They require willpower, which I sadly lack when I wake up in the morning. They take up valuable time which I would prefer to spend lolling in a bath, dawdling over breakfast, or browsing through the morning paper. I do them chiefly for negative reasons—because without them I feel depressed and miserable, because I get stiff-jointed, slow-moving, dull-thinking and finally end up with disc or sacro-iliac trouble. These exercises suit me because, unless I am living with some great extra stress, I can keep fit with no more than thirty minutes a day spent on them. They give me a rosy view of life and make me feel ready for action. If you try them, I believe you will find the same thing.

How do you feel when you wake up in the morning? In this year, 1968, I usually wake up feeling depressed. I am reluctant to get up or do anything, and yet I know that if I lie in bed I shall only become more depressed. So I rally all the willpower I can muster, get up and start doing my breathing exercises. Life stirs. I do more exercises. The stretching and physical effort starts vitality creeping through my veins. At the end of my half-hour's regime, I feel alive and the prospect of troubles and worries is one that I feel I can battle with. Presently I am feeling healthy enough to wish that I could add a walk, a run or a swim to my half-hour's activity.

I am sure it is against nature to do any exercise unless forced to it. A man may willingly walk to get food if he is hungry but it requires strength of mind to walk for exercise. The reason for doing any particular exercise is usually a negative one; for instance, a powerful reason for exercising stomach muscles is the negative one of avoiding a pot-belly, and the sight of someone waddling along with such a thing is probably the best inducement to continue doing half an hour's exercises every day, however reluctantly.

I have tried out, or considered, many different sets of exercises described in many books, and the ones I now use are those I think best.

I believe that Yoga is, taken as a whole, the best system of exercising. Yoga exercises are included in most sets that I have read about and I have included several in my regime. I strongly recommend anyone who wishes to do more than my half-hour regime to find a Yoga instructor or study some of the books on Yoga. I am convinced, however, that great caution is needed by a Westerner who tackles some of the Yoga poses and exercises. An Oriental used to them from childhood can find them easy and beneficial in cases where a Westerner, trying them for the first time, may seriously hurt himself, if his muscles have lost their elasticity or his body is not supple.

In some of the Yoga exercises I use, I have modified several movements or poses which I think unsuitable for someone who has not had much practice, or who has not the guidance of an instructor.

I suppose I am lucky in that, when I was eight, a good foundation was laid for a successful daily regime of exercises to-day. At my preparatory school, The Old Ride, we were drilled in exercises for twenty minutes every morning. Standing in front of us, the Headmaster, S. A. Phillips, conducted the pantomime. He was of podgy build and may well have had his own figure in mind when he persisted in this daily drill; but now I look on him as a benefactor. I am sure that when I switched from a fully active physical life to a sedentary one with heavy demands on nervous energy and brain work, I could have achieved far more than I have done if I had stuck to S.A.P.'s regime.

I do all the exercises I have described in thirty minutes, but of course I am used to them. When I last timed them, they took me 26½ minutes one day and 25½ minutes the next. Anyone starting on them would take longer at first. I suggest working through the list for thirty minutes and leaving the remainder for the next day. Don't rush and don't take it all too seriously. You will be doing them to make life more pleasant, so don't rush at them, straining and groaning like a galley slave. If you need to cut down the number of exercises so as not to exceed thirty minutes, choose the ones you like best and the ones you need most.

When describing an exercise I frequently use the word 'you', as if telling you to do the exercise. Strictly speaking I ought always to use the pronoun 'I' because I am describing an exercise as I do it; but it is so boring to read a text peppered with 'I's, that I keep on switching over to 'you's.

If you do these exercises, you must take great care never to strain yourself in any way. If you have any weakness in any organ, joint or muscle, you should consult your doctor before tackling an exercise which could be hurtful.

The following points apply to many, if not all, of the exercises.

Stretching. When stretching is prescribed after an exercise, lie on the floor, stretch fully with arms behind your head and straight. Your toes should be turned up and stretching in the direction of your chin. Stretch until you feel it through your whole body. Then relax everything completely.

Relaxing. Run your thoughts over your joints and muscles, to check that they are all relaxed and free from any tension. It will help if you review in turn toe joints, ankles, leg muscles, knees, thighs, hips—all these first for one leg and then the other. Then think of all the vertebrae in your spine, starting from the tail and ending at the neck. Usually, if you discover that there is tension at some point along this route, it is easy to relax that tension. I have read that you cannot consciously relax; you can only learn to let go. I think you will find that by one means or the other you can end up relaxed as long as you notice first that you are tense. After the spine there are the fingers, wrists, elbows and shoulder joints, also the muscles along the arm. Your belly muscles are especially important. Your jaw muscles, and even muscles at the base of your ears can be tense at times. Having checked that your whole body is relaxed and free from any tension, stay relaxed for at least a few seconds, and up to a minute, if you feel that it is doing you good and you can manage it.

Ability to relax completely is a wonderful asset, invaluable for a healthy mind and mental outlook as well as for physical wellbeing. As a general rule, relax after every exercise. In the end it will become an effortless habit.

Judging time. You can judge twenty seconds nearly enough by counting, 'and one, and two, and three,' etc. Try this a few times, timing your count against a watch. You will be surprised how accurately you can measure time with a little practice.

The exact length of time spent on any one exercise is not important. If you think that you should spend more time on a particular exercise, do so. I have set them out in the order which I recommend, keeping the more tricky ones at the end, but frequently I change the order, or do an exercise twice instead of once as prescribed.

Exercise 1

First, stand, heels together, arms at side of body.

Breathe in steadily and quietly until your lungs feel full. Your chest should swell visibly. Try to draw air into the bottom of your lungs.

When you think your lungs are full, lift your arms slowly sideways to overhead. This will enable you to draw in a little more air as if the arms acted like a pump. Stretch upwards.

Remain in this position holding your breath for a second. (After practice you can hold the position for longer; I hold it for seven seconds.)

Lower your arms slowly in front of you, bending forward, while breathing out steadily without effort. Continue the bending movement until your fingers point to your toes. If you are supple enough you can touch the floor without bending your knees, but don't strain.

As your lungs feel empty, draw in your stomach so as to press on the bottom of your lungs with your diaphragm and expel yet more air.

When you have a natural desire to breathe in again, rise and assume the standing position. Relax for a few seconds. Now proceed with the second part of this exercise as follows:

Place the palms of your hands against your lower ribs, spreading the fingers over the ribs so that the fingertips come more or less to the ends of the ribs in front.

Breathe in quietly and steadily until the chest has filled out. Feel the lower ribs pressing gently against your hands. As you get used to this exercise you will be able to move your belly, as if expanding it, to draw air into the bottom of your lungs.

Breathe out steadily, pressing your diaphragm upwards to expel the air from your lungs, until they seem empty.

Finally press gently inwards with your hands on the ribs to expel yet more air.

Repeat the whole sequence three times if your lungs are in good condition. My lungs are not in good order at present and I not only do the exercise seven times but repeat the second part of it at other times during the day.

The longer you take over the breathing sequence, the better, provided you do not strain at holding your breath. I take 25 seconds over the first part of the exercise and 20 seconds over the second part with 5–10 seconds between them.

Full breathing

Deep breathing is the most important exercise of all. Many people, after they leave school, go through life without ever exercising their lungs fully, without ever stretching their lungs. Nature's law is inexorable—any part of the body which is not used will atrophy in time. Though it may take many generations to complete the process, it starts at once and ends in the unused part or organ disappearing through evolution or else through disease.

I like to exercise my lungs fully every day and besides this I like to run, walk or climb stairs till I am panting. If I am in good nick, I run upstairs until panting. This sets the blood pulsating through all the lung tissue and makes the lung work hard to draw as much oxygen as possible from the air breathed in. No one should attempt this unless sure his or her heart is sound and strong enough for it.

Lungs are very important because, firstly, one cannot feel well if they are not functioning properly, and, secondly, they are apt to be seriously neglected and insufficiently used because of our inactive life to-day. I believe that the first exercise of this half-hour programme is sufficient to keep your lungs fit if they are fit to start with. If, however, they have been neglected for years and you have had serious trouble with them, it may be advisable to repeat the exercise several times a day.

The great efficacy of this breathing exercise will be obvious if you have any catarrh, phlegm or mucus in your lungs. It will start you coughing until this stuff is expelled from the extremities of the lung tissue and worked out of the lungs with help from the ciliary hairs lining the bronchial tubes. These, if the lungs are healthy, will expel the stuff just as waves cast flotsam on to a beach.

Never feel over-strained with this exercise. If coughing too much, stop for a while and try again after doing some of the other exercises.

The second part of the exercise is a quick one compared with the others. It massages and exercises the little-used lung tissue at the bottom and sides of the lungs.

Exercise 2

If deep breathing makes you feel short of breath, as if you are beginning to suffocate for want of oxygen, try the following which I have found to give amazing relief at times.

Place a fingertip under each side of the nose and press firmly. While continuing to press with the fingers, move them outwards towards the cheek bones while you breathe through your nose. This inhibits or checks the spasm in the lung which causes the choking feeling or shortness of breath. It is similar in effect to stopping a sneeze by pressing under your nose with a finger—a well-known nursery trick.

While pressing thus with the fingertips, breathe in and out through the nose as in the second part of the exercise, namely:

Breathe out steadily, pressing your diaphragm upwards to expel the air from your lungs, until they seem quite empty.

When you feel a natural urge to inhale, breathe in quietly and steadily until the chest has filled out and the belly expanded to let air draw into the bottom of the lungs.

This can be repeated 10 times; and again whenever you feel the need for it throughout the day.

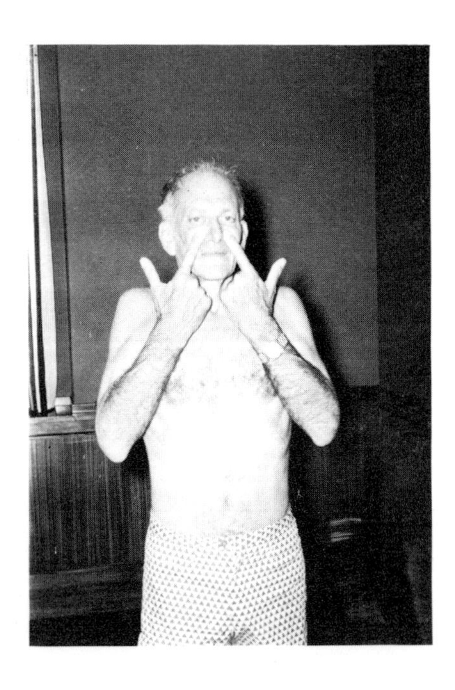

Roon's exercise

I was introduced to Roon's breathing exercise by Dr. Gordon Latto. Mrs. Karin Roon was a refugee from Germany who settled in the U.S.A. and helped thousands of asthmatics with this breathing 'trick'.

Exercise 3

Lie on your back, fully stretched out, with arms reaching behind your head, and legs straight.
Stretch fully, then relax every joint for a few seconds.*
Sit up on the floor.
Double up your right leg to bring the heel into your groin, with the sole of the foot against the inside of the left thigh. If necessary, you can guide your foot with your hands, but don't strain any muscle.
Bend forwards until your face is touching your left knee, or as close to it as is comfortable. Your forearms should be on the floor, your fingers reaching for your left heel. When supple, you can touch the heel with your fingers.
Stay in this position for a count of twenty seconds.
Repeat the exercise for the other leg.
Lie flat and stretch the whole body from fingertips to toes.
Relax everything and lie limp all over for a few seconds.

* See page 20 for a full description of stretching and relaxing.

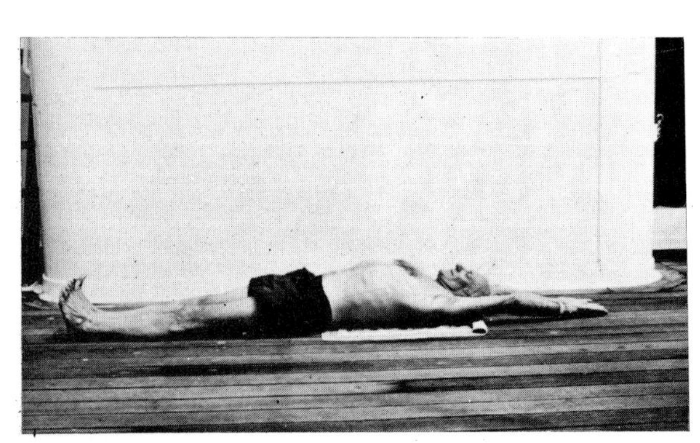

General stretch

When first this exercise is done, you may not be supple enough or have enough control of your leg muscles to double up your leg and bring the heel into the groin. Take care not to strain any foot or ankle muscles. If it hurts or feels a strain to bring the heel right to the groin, let it rest on the floor as near as you can comfortably get it, while you bend your head down to the other leg, which is the main object of the exercise. The picture shows the position to be achieved after some practice. Don't expect to get there first time.

Exercise 4

Lie on your back, arms on the floor and stretched out straight behind your head (i.e. beyond the back of your head), thumbs together, palms up.

Lift your legs slowly, keeping them straight, unbent. Move them through the vertical position and on until the toes touch the tips of your fingers on the floor or as near them as you can comfortably reach. You should feel the lower spine stretching. Stay in this position for a count of twenty seconds.

Move your legs forward again and lower them to the floor as slowly as you comfortably can.

With arms on the floor, hands still beyond the back of your head, stretch from fingertips to toes before relaxing everything and lying quite limp for five seconds.

Spine exercise

This is an excellent exercise for the lower part of the spine, making it supple and stretching it. It is also excellent for the stomach, which is massaged by the tautening of the muscles when the legs are raised or lowered slowly. When you feel these muscles as hard as wood you may well be confident that you have here the best preventive of a pot belly or of constipation.

Exercise 5

Lie on a towel or mat spread on the floor; face down, chin on the floor, arms at sides.

Raise your head and shoulders off the floor, arms still at sides, curving your spine backwards as much as you comfortably can. Be aware of muscles taking an even strain all along the spine from hips to head. (When you have mastered this attitude, raise your legs and feet off the floor at the same time, so that your body is curved from head to foot with only your belly and thighs touching the floor.)

Make an effort to hold this attitude for five seconds.

Now plant your hands, one palm under each shoulder, elbows outwards, and take the weight of your upper body on them. Straighten your arms and stretch your spine in an upward curve.

Lower and raise your body an inch or two until you feel the spine being stretched between adjacent vertebrae right along it.

Remain with spine stretched and curved for a count of twenty seconds.

Lower your body slowly and lie completely relaxed, cheek on floor, for from twenty seconds up to a minute.

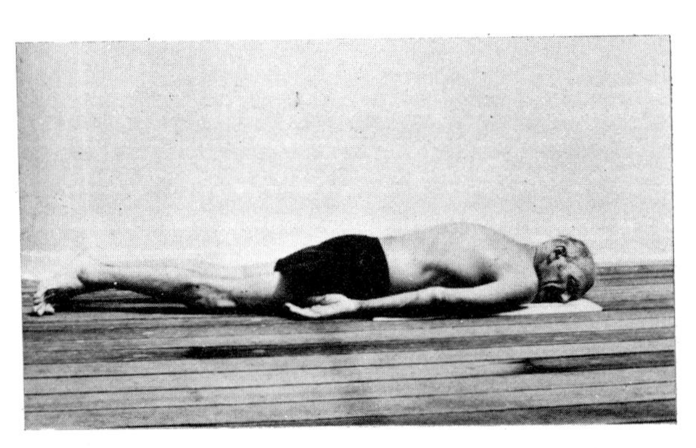

Curved back

With your elbows out, fingers pointing inwards and head up, you may feel like an iguana or lizard peering ahead; no matter, on with the job. I find that by raising or lowering myself a little by bending my arms, I can feel the stretch taking effect right along the spine. Also, while doing this, I turn my head a little first to one side and then to the other. It seems as if the effect can be felt on every one of the vertebrae. The value of this exercise and the others that work on the spine is immense. Before I started exercising my spine in this deliberate way, I used to have disc or sacroiliac trouble nearly every spring, at the end of an inactive winter following a strenuous summer. Anyone who has had this trouble knows what agony it can be and how at least it immobilises one for days. While I have done these exercises, I have had no further attack of disc trouble, thank God.

Exercise 6

This is to stand on your shoulders and the back of your head.

From lying full length, first raise your legs to an upright position, then raise the lower part of your body to as near the vertical as you comfortably can while keeping your legs vertical. Your upper arms, flat on the floor, will help you to balance on your shoulders and the back of your head. Your spine should be curving from the neck where it is horizontal to the bottom of the spine where it is vertical. If necessary prop the small of your back with your palms, as if you had your hands on the back of your hips.

Remain standing on your shoulders while you thoroughly relax. I recommend this for as long as you like up to two minutes.

Lower your legs and body slowly to the floor. Stretch at full length, then completely relax every joint and muscle for five seconds.

Standing on your shoulders

This is a valuable relaxing exercise. You can feel worry oozing away as you stay inverted. I believe the reason for this is that worry or strain tenses your muscles and hinders the easy circulation of blood. Turning your body upside down brings the blood into the head under some pressure. If you are sceptical about this, a simple experiment will convince you; simply look at your fingers and note their colour, which should be pink or flesh-coloured, then stretch your arms above your head and keep them there a while, say, half a minute. Now look at your fingers again; they will be ashen or near white because the blood has drained out of them. And so, when you invert your body, the blood tends to drain from the legs and body into your head, shoulders and lungs. When you stand up again, it will drain back.

After this exercise, stretch at full length on the floor as usual and then relax everything for a few seconds before the next exercise.

Exercise 7

From lying on the floor, arms at sides, rise slowly to sitting upright.
With arms stretched straight in front, continue bending your body until it is doubled up, head down, face on or near your knees, fingers reaching for your heels. When supple enough, the ideal position is to have your face resting on your knees, forearms along the floor, fingers hooked under your feet.
Remain in this position for a count of twenty seconds.
Slowly rise to sitting position, arms straight over your head.
Continue moving your body back until at full length on the floor, arms straight out beyond your head.
Stretch from fingertips to toes and then relax every joint and muscle for five seconds.

Stretch and be supple

If your spine is too stiff some mornings to bring face down to knees, you will find that, by holding to the position reached each time you breathe in, your spine will bend a little more and your head will drop a little each time you breathe out. In the end your head will probably come down quite easily to touch the knees.

If you find at first that you cannot double up enough, you must not strain to do so. You will find you get noticeably more supple after a few days.

Proper suppleness will enable you to clasp your heels, or at least touch them with your fingers, while your forearms lie on the floor beside your legs. But don't worry if you can't do all this at first. You can't expect to be as supple as a teenager all at once if you have been neglecting your body for years. You will be surprised how suppleness will come if you have the strength of mind to keep exercising half an hour a day for a few weeks to achieve it.

This excellent exercise is similar to No. 2, but more effective in stretching the whole spine and making it supple, strengthening the stomach muscles and, in doing so, massaging the stomach. One's inside should work as regularly and as easily as a clock if one does the exercises in this half-hour daily course; but if you wish to tone up the action of your stomach, you can repeat this particular exercise up to six times. Once a day is enough to keep you fit once you are fit.

Exercise 8

Sit upright, legs apart on the floor and straight in front of you.

Double up the left leg to bring the left heel against the right groin. You can lift it in with your hands if necessary, but if so take great care not to strain or pull a muscle.

Double up the other leg across the left shinbone to bring the right heel to the groin with the sole of the foot against the inside of the left thigh. After some practice of getting into this position, your body will be supple enough to allow the outer side of each leg and knee to lie flat on the floor.

Body upright, hands lightly on your knees, you can relax motionless, your mind a blank (if you wish); and for as long as you wish. I use this attitude while doing neck, eye, shoulder and ear exercises which follow on.

If you cannot manage this position (and it would be unusual to achieve it at once), sit in the ordinary cross-legged position, buttock on heel.

The cross-legged pose

This cross-legged pose resembles the Buddha's sitting attitude, which is such a favourite in Yoga exercises. There is an important difference, however, which I will discuss, because I believe the Buddha pose can be dangerous for a Westerner to attempt except under the eye of an accomplished instructor. In the Buddha pose each heel is resting against the stomach *on top* of the opposite thigh. Orientals who have practised this attitude since childhood have no difficulty with it but it is unnatural for a middle-aged Westerner. I used it for some time but it strained and slackened sinews in my ankles. This was due to my own fault of being determined to master immediately a pose unsuitable for me. (My ankles have been damaged many times in crashes and accidents.)

The Buddha attitude is marvellously conducive to relaxing and thence meditating, but also the position I have described for this exercise is excellent for relaxing the mind as well as the muscles.

Much has been written about the great benefit of meditation. Yoga disciples remain motionless in the Buddha pose for long periods, relaxed and meditating. Anyone with an urge to meditate should be encouraged to seek expert instruction from a master of Yoga. In this programme of exercises lasting only thirty minutes, there is no time for it or place to discuss it.

Exercise 9

Sit upright, cross-legged.

Tip your head back, feeling your neck stretch fully but without strain. Remain in this and the succeeding positions just long enough to feel the stretching effect before proceeding with the next movement.

Tip your head forward until the chin is pressing against the chest.

Turn the head to the left until you feel the twist of the neck acting on the spine; then slowly turn it to the right. Stretch but don't strain; the object is to make your neck supple.

Let your head loll over from upright towards your left shoulder, until your ear touches the shoulder. If unable to bring your ear down to the shoulder, raise the shoulder to close the gap. Keep as relaxed as you can while doing this.

At this point, to make my neck and spine more supple, I place the fingers of my left hand on top of my head, touching my right ear, and I press the head gently down (towards the left shoulder if it is not already touching it) until I feel the vertebrae stretching sideways. Always remember the cardinal rule: 'stretch but don't strain'.

Repeat with the head lolling on the right shoulder.

Neck exercise

You must keep your neck muscles supple and your neck vertebrae pliant and well loosened up if you are to feel fit and keep your youthful enjoyment of life. The importance of a supple spine has been recognised for ages. In the Old Testament of the Bible, complaints are frequently made of people or persons being 'stiff-necked'.

Make all the movements of this exercise slowly and hold each attitude until you feel the neck vertebrae nicely stretched each time the neck is being bent or twisted.

Exercise 10 Eye exercise

Sit cross-legged on the floor, body upright, hands on knees in a relaxed attitude.

Move your head around clockwise in as large a circle as you can comfortably make.

In time with this head movement, roll your eyes round so that your line of sight is following as big a circle as possible with comfort. For example, if your head is turned fully to the left, you will be looking out of the left-hand corners of your eyes at the same instant.

You may notice that your line of sight moves in a series of jerks when tracing out the circle. Do not be alarmed, it always moves in jerks, but this is not usually noticed when looking straight ahead.

Make three circles slowly clockwise, followed by three more in the opposite direction.

This eye exercise appears to be partly a neck exercise. The fact is that any neck exercise is good for the eyes. If the nerves and muscles of the spine are in an unhealthy state, such as stiff or clogged with acid, eyesight is almost certain to suffer.

Good eyesight is rare without a supple neck and a pliant upper spine. The increasingly long sight which troubles people as they get older is usually due to the eye muscles stiffening up through lack of use until the eye focus cannot be adjusted by the stiff muscles. I find this exercise noticeably improves my own short sight. Without it I should need special spectacles for reading.

Exercise 11 Focusing exercise

While sitting cross-legged, body upright, hold a pin-point or pencil-point at arm's length.
Focus to see it as clearly as possible.
Move it slowly towards the face, keeping it in focus. See how near your nose you can keep it in focus. When it looks blurred, move it out slowly to arm's length again.
Repeat three times. Note after a week what improvement it has had on your sight.

Exercise 12 Shoulder exercise

Sit cross-legged, body upright. Work your shoulderblades, both together, round in as large a circle as you can.

Crook your arms at the elbows to keep them clear of the floor, but otherwise keep your arms limp.

Repeat seven times, rotating your shoulders in one direction, followed by seven times in the opposite direction.

The speed of the movement is not important, but you should be conscious of making as big a circle as possible all the way round.

Exercise 13 Ear exercise

Sit cross-legged, body upright.
Insert the tip of the small finger into each ear and wiggle it for five seconds so as to make a drumming sound.
This must be done carefully, because ear drums are so delicate.

This exercise is to loosen up the muscles of the middle ear which are apt to lose their resilience through insufficient use, thus impairing the hearing.

My hearing is noticeably better after a simulated yawn, as used in a climbing aircraft to relieve the pressure building up behind the ear drums. Sometimes I give my ear drums a stretch by holding my nose while I gently increase breath pressure in the tubes to the ear. This is used in a descending aircraft to relieve the pressure outside the ear drums.

My hearing is poor in one ear; I have great difficulty in hearing a person speaking to me from close-to if there is a lot of noise around as at a cocktail or dinner party. I notice that when listening to a dawn chorus of birds, I can hear birds like pigeons equally well with my bad ear, while it cannot at all hear other birds like sparrows. I used to think my hearing was damaged by sitting for hours in an open cockpit subjected to the roar of the open exhaust stubs a few feet in front of me. But why should this damage one ear and not the other? Perhaps one ear drum was damaged while boxing, or in an accident.

Exercise 14

Sit on the floor, legs together in front of you.

Lean back, supporting yourself with arms straight from shoulders to floor, palms on the floor.

Crook your knees, drawing your heels to within a foot of your buttocks.

Lift your bottom off the floor and swing it forward against your heels. You are now supported by your hands and feet.

Walk your body forward on your palms, a few inches at a time, so that your knees move forward and downwards until they rest on the floor. You are now kneeling on the floor with your arms straight up and down supporting your shoulders.

Move your head back as far as you comfortably can so that your spine is arched upwards. Feel it stretching in an upward bow for five seconds.

Now inch your body forwards, using your hands (or fingers, if necessary) on the floor to do so, until you can squat on your heels.

Stay in this position, balanced on your toes, for five seconds, before rising slowly by straightening your legs.

Spine arching

With the spine curved upwards, it is being stretched in a different way.
The squatting position before rising is good for the balancing muscles of your feet.

Exercise 15

Place a pad like a folded handkerchief or face flannel two feet from a suitable wall.
Bend down, head towards the wall, so as to place the top of your forehead on the pad.
Place your clasped fingers over the top of your head just above your forehead. They are then between the top of your head and the pad.
Keep your forearms on the floor, elbows out to each side, to enable you to balance sideways while standing on your head.
Walk your toes towards your face, an inch or two at a 'step', until your body is doubled up, knees to chest, body upright and upside down.
Lift your feet off the ground slowly and raise your legs into the air.
Straighten your legs slowly, until they are straight above your body, and you are balanced on your head.
If uncertain of your balance at first, keep your legs bent so that your feet touch the wall behind you. You will then feel secure against toppling over backwards or sideways. If you should begin to topple forwards, double up your legs so as to land on your toes, the natural way to return from the upside-down position.
Remain on your head as relaxed as possible, trying to keep your mind at ease and preferably blank. At first you should hold this position for only a few seconds. After some weeks when you are thoroughly accustomed to it, you can hold it as long as you like provided you feel comfortable and unstrained, for up to three minutes.
At the end of the exercise double up to bring your knees close to your body. Take care to keep your legs close to your body as you lower your feet to the floor so that they will not land with a jarring impact.

Standing on your head

This is one of the most important exercises, but should not be attempted unless your circulatory system is normal. Stated briefly, it is little more than standing on your head while keeping a relaxed attitude of mind. I suppose this must seem to many people a strange thing to do. If it seems so to you, I suggest you keep an open mind until you have actually tried it and have had actual experience of its effect. It is an effective physical means of easing worry or of removing it completely for some time.

I always do this exercise with a wall two feet from my back so that I cannot fall over backwards if I lose my balance. I suppose this would be quite unnecessary if I had learned the exercise when I was young.

Having practised this exercise for a long time, I remain in the upside-down position, as relaxed as possible and trying to keep my mind blank, for up to three minutes. As the blood floods into my head and the upper parts of my body I begin to feel peaceful. Things that enraged, exasperated or worried me will take their right value and seem trivial compared with the pleasure and importance of carefree living. If you do it I believe you will gradually feel more at peace with your life. Calm steals through your body and after that follows a slow surge of vitality, until you feel not only full of life but happy too.

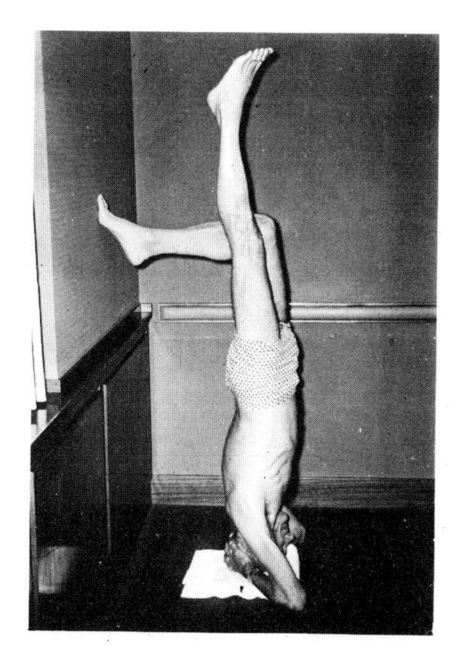

Exercise 16 Spine stretched sideways

Stand upright, feet together, arms level and outstretched sideways.

Bend sideways to the right, raising your left arm above your head and stretching it over your head to the right so as to stretch your spine in a curve as far to the right as you possibly can. At the same time keep your eye on the little finger of your left hand, this will result in curving your neck well too. Stretch your right arm downwards beside your body to help to curve the spine to the right.

Remain in this attitude, outstretched, for a count of seven seconds.

Repeat, bending to the left.

Previous spine exercises have been stretching the spine backwards or forwards; this one stretches it to each side.

Exercise 17 Twisting the spine

Stand upright, feet together, arms stretched out in front, straight and level, thumbs together.

Without moving the feet, turn or twist the body slowly to the right as far as you can without strain. At the same time, turn your head to the right as far as you comfortably can, keeping your eye on the little finger of your right hand.

Hold this posture, feeling the twist all along your spine for a count of ten seconds.

Repeat, twisting to the left.

When used to this exercise, do it while on your toes. It will then be good also for your balancing muscles.

This exercise completes the batch aiming to stretch your spine every way, to twist it, and make it thoroughly supple. After lungs, the spine is probably the most neglected part of the body. And it is one of the most important. If you start with stiff spine and vertebrae jammed and stuck together, you will be amazed at the feeling of lightness and agility you will gain after a few days of these exercises. The old test of touching the floor with your fingers while bending over, keeping the knees quite straight, should seem child's play. You will probably be able to stretch over to lay your palms on the floor, still keeping your knees unbent.

Exercise 18 Walking straight-legged

Walk across the room, stiff-legged, that is with knees stiff and unbent, keeping your toes cocked up as far off the floor as you can raise them. If possible, walk on the heels only.
Neglected muscles will ache as you try to bend your toes upwards.
Return across the room on tiptoe.
Repeat twice.

I think everyone must have a weakness in his body which needs special attention. For instance, in my own case my ankles have been damaged time after time, including breaks due to my seaplane crash in 1931 and while ski-ing in Austria, and a bad sprain in New Zealand with twelve hours of rough going among hills and along a river bed after the sprain. In 1966 a heavy fall on the deck of *Gipsy Moth IV* ended in my being unable to walk more than a few paces because some muscles in the left foot and leg were paralysed or out of action. It was not till fourteen months after this accident that I set to work on the damaged leg, that is to say not until I finished my solo voyage round the world, and by then some of the muscles seemed to have atrophied. However, after exercising that leg every morning for eight months, I was able to walk up to a mile fairly fast, though the foot movement was still a little abnormal. By keeping at it I expect to have the foot quite normal again in time. As a result of all this, I do more foot and leg exercises than I otherwise would. I suggest you decide for yourself how many you should do.

I think it is worth while exercising enough to keep a good sense of balance, if only for the negative reason that it may save you from falls due to lack of balance.

When I first started this exercise I could not lift the toes of my damaged leg off the floor at all, and it seemed that I never would be able to do so, but after eight months of exercising they all lifted off, though only half as high as those of the undamaged foot.

Exercise 19 Foot circling

Balance on the left foot, swing the right leg forward, leg straight. Hold this attitude while doing the exercise. In the picture I am holding on to the porthole because the ship was rolling.
Rotate the right foot seven times clockwise. Describe as big a circle in the air with the toes as you can.
Repeat, standing on the right foot and rotating the other foot.
Repeat with both feet but with an anti-clockwise circling movement.

Many muscles will be stretched by this exercise, and, if they ache, it will show that they have been neglected.

Exercise 20 Ankle exercise

Balance on the left foot, right leg forward, leg straight.
Using only the ankle joint, turn the sole of the right foot first outwards as far as you can and then inwards.
Repeat seven times.
Repeat with the other foot.

The movement is such that if the foot were on the floor, it would touch only along the outside or the inside of the foot, according to which way the ankle has been turned.

Exercise 21 Foot exercise

Balance on the left foot, right leg forward and straight.
Turn up the right foot and toes as far as you can. You will probably feel the tendons under your knee taking the strain.
Turn the foot down so that the toes point down at the floor.
Repeat this seven times with the right foot.
Repeat seven times with the left foot.

The very best of luck to all my readers who try out these exercises!

Fasting

I can only record the beneficial effect that a fast has on myself. As I am not a doctor, I cannot recommend treatment for others or claim that it will benefit anyone else.

For me fasting is the most effective beneficial treatment that I have ever experienced. I am not attempting to explain why; it is advocated and discussed continually in nature cure journals, naturopathic journals and books. I keep for reference Alan Moyle's book, *Nature Cure Explained,* which was given to each patient at Enton Hall Nature Cure Hydro when I was there recovering from my lung trouble. Moyle's chapter 'Why Fast?' is excellent. He describes a number of fasts for different ailments, reasons or persons.

The fast I use mostly (and fairly regularly too) is called the Guelpa, after the renowned Italian who developed it. He called it a cure because even on the first day, when fruit juice is drunk, the fast is not absolute. Experience has led me to modify details of it, as I have found one variation or another more effective.

The Guelpa is laid down by Alan Moyle as a three-day fast, but I have found that a two-day version is all I need. This is the only fast in which an aperient is used to rid the body of toxins quickly. It enables the fast to be completed during a weekend without interrupting the normal work of the week.

I do not like fasting, I hate it. I find it grim and depressing to wake up in the morning and think, "No food at all to-day." This is only due to being brought up to eat three meals a day, and to this becoming a habit so strong that fasting produces a craving like that of an addict deprived of tobacco, drink or drug. Not only does this craving vanish after about two days of fasting, but after another day or two's fast a dislike of food begins to develop, which could become dangerous after a long fast of, say, thirty days. Do not be scared, I am going to describe a fast of only two days' duration.

I do not like fasting if seriously ill because then eating becomes one of the few remaining consolations in a miserable existence and I look forward to the next feed even if I can't enjoy it when it comes.

The best time to fast is when content to lie about doing nothing, when not wanting to meet people or mix with them when they are eating.

I find that if I have delayed a needed fast too long, I get a nasty gnawing headache above one eye or at the back of my head, and have a furry white tongue; this is due to the toxins being stirred up in the body by the fast. I know it is nonsense hating to start a fast, especially when there is no real hardship as in the case of the Guelpa, where one is allowed to drink apple-juice at intervals of a few hours throughout the first day.

During this fast I eat nothing the first day and drink only apple-juice. (For the best effect the apple-juice should be freshly squeezed from apples, but for convenience I drink Schloer, which has not much preservative in it.)

I drink no more after I have gone to bed at the end of the first day. I do not expect to sleep as well as usual. If I wake in the middle of the night and have difficulty in getting off to sleep again, I usually start on the second day's regime by eating some dry toast.

In the second half of this regime I do without any drink at all for thirty-six hours except for one glass of wine which I will explain later. During this dry period I eat nothing at all except dry toast which should be dried in an oven to extract nearly all the moisture from it. Sometimes I use French *biscottes,* which I fear may not be quite as good but which are certainly nice and palatable. The object of the dry toast is to absorb liquid in the body while triggering off the action of the kidneys (or, in my case, the kidney). As the liquid available in the body gets used up, the kidney, being short of liquid to work on, begins to draw acid from the body.

At six or seven in the evening I drink a glass of white wine. This has a magic action in making the kidney intensify its raid on the acid stored in the body.

On the morning of the third day a glass of good, cold water is like nectar; but I try not to drink more than I badly need that day because the kidney action will continue to get rid of acid for most of the day, if the body tissue is not re-saturated with liquid.

All the textbooks say that a fast must be followed by several days of partial fasting. I regret that I am weak and self-indulgent about this; feeling wonderfully fit, I have an urge to resume life at full blast at once, which I know is wrong.

This fast is drastic treatment, as shown by my losing 6½ to 8½ pounds' weight each time. My doctor seemed a little apprehensive about it. He often prescribes a dry day only but I find that in my case this does not get rid of acid without the preliminary fruit-juice day.

There is one most important point for me about fasting— on no account must I make any business decision or agreement for several days afterwards. My judgment is always rotten at the end of a fast because I feel so strong and full of vitality, so sanguine and optimistic, so happy and benevolent, that projects which seemed difficult or dangerous before fasting now seem simple, easy and safe. At the same time I become intolerant and impatient; I cannot bear to be held up from action for a moment and, if thwarted or kept waiting, am likely to fly into a temper or rush into doing something rash, when I ought to be thinking, considering and pondering first. But the normal routine of living returns only too soon. Perhaps I should add that I do not believe this Guelpa fast is any good for reducing fat. The body is so healthy after it that it puts on weight again easily.

Here is the description of the fast in the form in which I undertake it:

1st day: Fruit-juice day

On waking take half an ounce of Epsom salts in sufficient warm water to dissolve it. Drink half a pint of warm water immediately afterwards.

Repeat this dose half an hour later.

At mealtimes, and, if desired, at mid-morning or mid-afternoon, drink apple-juice.

Drink nothing more after turning in for the night.

2nd day: Dry day

Drink nothing from the time of going to bed on the first day to the time of getting up on the third day, except one glass of white wine at about six o'clock on the second day.

During this period eat nothing except very dry toast.

Diet

I prefer to eat vegetarian food because I believe I keep more healthy when I stick to it, and I am quite sure that it has several times been a major cause of my recovering from illness. I believe this is because a man's inside, with its thirty feet of gut, is designed to digest fruit, nuts and vegetables but is not well-suited for meat, especially if that is not fresh when it starts on its long voyage through man's interior. I used to eat a lot of meat when I was young and only gave up doing so when I was put on to a nature-cure routine to get rid of gallstone trouble. I still eat fish when I am dining out and enjoy it occasionally. I believe that man can eat almost anything as long as he does not eat much of it, and provided that he eats at the same time as much as his body must have to provide him with the various vitamins etc. Adelle Davis records the finding by physicians at Cornell (U.S.A.) University Medical School, that the human stomach would deal with any material classified as edible which could be swallowed, including (oh, be joyful, I say!) 100 per cent. alcohol. Often it is not what you eat but what you feel which causes illness. Any strong negative emotion such as rage, resentment, fear or dread, floods the stomach with acid. If food is eaten soon after this has happened, it will be wrongly blamed for the illness caused sooner or later. Time after time Dr. Latto has advised me not to eat for three hours after an emotional upset. I believe the most important rule of diet is to eat little and chew it much; it is so often stated that a man who lives to a great age and keeps fit eats little and never indulges in anything to excess. I agree, but at the same time I believe it is sometimes worth paying the price to indulge in a gorgeous project to glorious excess.